Peacefully Reflect & Abide in Yahweh (PRAY)

A Guided Devotional Prayer Journal

Seeking God Club

INDEPENDENT AUTHORS PUBLICATIONS

Independent Authors Publications

Roselle, New Jersey

Peacefully Reflect & Abide in Yahweh (PRAY)

A Guided Devotional Prayer Journal

Copyright © 2021 by Seeking God Club

Independent Authors Publications
P.O Box 7062
Roselle, NJ 07203
www.independentauthorspublications.com

Books may be ordered through booksellers or publisher by contacting us on our website.

Printed in the United States of America
First Printing, 2021

Book Cover Design – Humbird Media
Editor – Catherine Felegi
Book Formatter – Polgarus Studio

ISBN 978-1-950974-02-3 (paperback)

Endorsement

In Psalms 63:1 New International Version, David says, "You, God, are my God, earnestly I seek You…" The value of daily spiritual devotions cannot be underestimated. They are steps leading to greater things in your spiritual walk that impact your life and purpose as a whole. David, the shepherd boy, the giant killer, King of Israel, man after God's own heart, and author of 73 Psalms in the Old Testament, knew the value of seeking God daily. It was the source of his strength in the highs and the lows of his life. A lesson we all should follow daily.

Candi Young and the Seeking God Club have assembled a collection of daily devotions to challenge, inspire, and connect you to the heart of the Father, and give spiritual bread for the day's journey. Many of these devotions were birthed from personal challenges and experiences and shared especially for you. God's promise to us is, if we Seek Him, we will Find Him (Jeremiah 29:13), the key word being "seek", to search for something. Join the Seeking God Club through this daily journey as you seek God out and invite Him into your personal journey. Let these times of devotion lead you to greater heights in your relationship with Him.

Pastor Fred McCarthy
Oasis Christian Centre
Rahway, NJ

Acknowledgements

The Seeking God Club (SGC) would like to thank the leadership and support of Fred McCarthy, Lead Pastor at Oasis Christian Centre in Rahway, New Jersey. Many of us have spiritually grown and are fueled towards a higher purpose because of our connection with Oasis.

Blessings to Minister Jimmie L. McClendon for her affirming words of support, listening ear, and for being an avid contributor to our online community. Thank you for volunteering to facilitate over the years.

The Seeking God Club is grateful to our publisher, Renaee Smith from Independent Authors Publisher (IAP), and her team who patiently helped us turn our dream into reality.

Thank you to every reader of this journal and those who participate in the Seeking God Club - past, present, and future. We do what we do because of you! We pray you will be blessed as you read what the Lord has directed to be written.

Last, but certainly not least, a special thank you to all the contributing writers from the Seeking God Club and their families. The continued faith, dedication, obedience, perseverance, support, and love for God's people is admirable. I am pleased and honored to call you brothers and sisters! You inspire the Seeking God Club to go forth! Thank you for seeing the vision, even when it was difficult to articulate, and running with it. Love always to Charlotte, Ingrid, Jonathan, Joyce, Keila, Maria, Mirian, Veniss, and Vilma.
– Candi Young

Dedication

This journal is dedicated to YAHWEH, the Great and All-Knowing
I AM who brings all things into existence.

Dear Jane,

We hope and pray that you enjoy this devotional journal and that you receive all the blessings that God has for you and your family, and that you remember us when you read this book.

God bless you always

Love,
Jonathan & Ingrid

Contents

Foreword

I was a woman living in the shadow of other people's approval. While I appeared to be okay on the outside, inside, I was insecure and felt empty and hurt. My journey in life was not easy because of some of the decisions I made. I was looking for happiness and satisfaction from people and not God.

After becoming a mother of two beautiful daughters, I made the firm decision to instil good values in them by raising them up in church. Little did I know God was working on ME. I quickly learned that I am responsible for my happiness and the way I feel. My relationship with God changed for the better, and life started to improve. I made a decision to live my life according to the Word of God. As I self-reflected, I found that I had a strong desire to help others. My changed focus and behavior led to me becoming a certified Minister in April 2006. Once you allow Jesus in your life, He will begin a new work in you.

It is exciting to express my love for God through the Seeking God Club (SGC) by both being an active listener and a teacher. I have learned that if you surrender to God, He will direct your path. I actively surround myself with awe-inspiring Christians who share their love of God and through this connection, my life continues to evolve.

The writers of this journal reflect an amazing wealth of knowledge that has a positive impact on so many others. What's more important than having faith? Putting your faith to work and helping others around you apply it to their lives. Their words speak for itself. Their wisdom has moved others to higher heights. All of the talent that God has provided them is exhibited in their obedience and behavior. "But the fruit of the Spirit is love, joy, peace, forbearance, kindness, goodness, faithfulness, gentleness, and self-control…" (Galatians 5:22-23, New International Version).

You may be dealing with the issues of life, but with the Bible, inspirational words of encouragement, and prayer, you will develop a personal relationship with God. Let's maximize what God has planned for each of us as we take this journey through this journal.

Minister Jimmie L McClendon
Good News Sounds of Pentecost Church International
Newark, New Jersey

Introduction

The Seeking God Club (SGC) is a community of prayer warriors, leaders, intercessors, and God seekers who come together via a conference line as well as on social media to share and hear the Word of God. Psalm 63:1 inspires and motivates their work of spreading the Word of the Lord to all who can hear - "O God, You are my God; Early will I seek You; My soul thirsts for You; My flesh longs for You In a dry and thirsty land Where there is no water." (New King James Version)

The idea started as an inspired suggestion from Charlotte Diakite to host an encouraging call Wednesdays at 6:00 am for 15 minutes. The duration was six weeks during a virtual teaching journey through the Purpose Driven Life (PDL) book. The call served as a mid-week rest stop for participants to fuel themselves to keep going.

At the conclusion of PDL, there was a passion to continue. It was at the same time Candi Young, was charged by Loni Arce of Oasis Christian Centre to seek God in prayer for an answer on how to keep the women's ministry, Women of Worth (WOW), connected between monthly meetings. Candi reflected on a vision God laid on her heart years ago about a daily prayer line, thus SGC was birthed. During 2018, SGC gradually increased in leaders as well as days. By January 2019, SGC expanded to six days a week with over ten rotating leaders committed to the mission, including a Spanish speaking segment.

SGC is God's ministry and has been blessed in spite of challenges. The fruit of SGC's labor shows in its leaders' personal growth, as well as the growth of those who listen-in. It spiritually appears that during 2018 and 2019, God was preparing SGC to be in position for the 2020 pandemic. The group was able to continue feeding God's people without missing a beat. God sent an increase of listeners to be fed as in-person gathering means were shut down. SGC was "in position" for such a time as this. SGC gives all glory, honor, and praise to God for His leading, covering, and favor; humbly submitting all to the Lord!

You may find SGC online at https://www.facebook.com/groups/seekinggodclub. You may also send your prayer requests to sgcpray@gmail.com where a team of intercessors will pray with and for you. God Bless You!

My Prayer For You

"If you remain in me and my words remain in you, you may ask for anything you want and it will be granted." - John 15:7, New Living Translation

With a humble heart, I come before You and glorify You, Lord! I exalt You and praise Your Holy Name.

My Father, dwelling in the heavenly realms, I pray for our readers. May the glory of Your name be the foundation of their lives. May they look to You for wisdom and guidance while they commit their ways unto You and lean not on their own understanding. Be enthroned in their heart, always.

Give them renewed strength and courage as they continue in faith to press on and move forward on the straight and narrow path - the path that leads to life eternal.

Help and protect them, Lord, in their daily walk. Give them peace in the midst of the storms of life. Forgive them any wrongs they have done, as they themselves release forgiveness to those who have wronged them. With patience, may they wait on You for the answers to their prayers.

You, oh Lord, are their hope and salvation. You know the plans You have for them; plans to help them prosper and not to harm them, to give them hope and a future. Rescue them every time they face tribulations and keep them from evil. You are the provider of all they need each day. All good things come from You, and they will lack nothing.

Holy Spirit, bless them with eternal blessings and show them the goodness of God, today and always. Their life remains forever in the palm of Your hands and Your words in their heart.

You are the King who rules with power and glory forever. Grant this prayer, oh Lord. It is with praise and thanksgiving that I lift it up to Your throne of glory. Amen.

Maria Rivera

Record your Notes or Reflections:

According to the verse above, we have confidence that God grants our requests. What are you asking God for?
What is your prayer today?

_____

_____

_____

_____

_____

_____

Beauty in The Darkness

"I will give you hidden treasures, riches stored in secret places, so that you may know that I am the Lord, the God of Israel, who summons you by name." - Isaiah 45:3 New International Version

I reckon we've all had times of discouragement and disappointment; we're human and life happens. Usually we bounce back, and generally, those moments don't last for an extended time. But what happens when they do? What happens when the marital discord has been going on for months without any sign of relief, or the wayward child doesn't "come to himself" and return home?

I'm sure some, probably many of us, have found ourselves in a season of despair and darkness, especially in light of this global pandemic and quarantine. What do you do when you find yourself in a dark place?

We know that God is omnipresent and is in all things. We know that all things work for our good, so perhaps if we look from God's eyes, it might shed some light on the darkness we are facing right now.

I'm fascinated by nature and gardening, and God often uses them as an illustration to bring revelation. When we plant a seed and place it in the dirt, we wait with expectation that it will yield fruit. The seed is quarantined and its purpose manifests in the darkness of the soil. It's a private process. The same thing happens with a caterpillar tightly swaddled in its cocoon.

The most magnificent seed, the seed of creation, transforms within the privacy of the mother's womb, completely in the dark. God creates in the dark.

Perhaps those dark places are shaping you into a new creation. Envision your dark place as a birthing canal - tight, uncomfortable, and even painful, but beautiful on the other side.

Shadrach, Meshach, and Abed-Nego were thrown into the furnace but did not burn. Elijah hid in a cave and heard from the Lord in a quiet gentle voice, and Moses was transformed, alone on the mountain.

The dark places can open doors for intimate encounters with the Father. He will MAKE us lie down in green pastures and will lead us beside STILL waters. Be still!

God is for you and His plans are perfect in the noisy as well as dark places.

I pray the prayer Elijah prayed over his servant, that your eyes would be opened and that you would see the army sent to protect you in the midst of the darkness.

Joyce Travers-Johnson

Record your Notes or Reflections:
Take some time for yourself and sit still. Reflect on a difficult time you've had in the past and ask yourself, what's different now that you're on the other side?
Are you stronger?
Did you gain insight?

Beloved, if you're here, then you've gotten through!

_____

_____

_____

_____

_____

_____

_____

_____

_____

_____

_____

_____

_____

We Can Make a Difference

"No one will be able to stand against you all the days of your life. As I was with Moses, so I will be with you; I will never leave you nor forsake you." - Joshua 1:5, New International Version

How blessed we are to have a Father like Jehovah, walking hand in hand with Him and having Him as a guide walking in a world of adversity. He's the direction we are looking for. He's the way for us to stay on the right path.

God has given us a task to accomplish - to bring the gospel to all who seek His name and are lost along the way, not knowing what to do or how to reach their destination.

Many people walk aimlessly, so we fear that we will put into effect the diligence that God has entrusted to us. Let's start with those who are around us. You'll be amazed how many people around you are looking for something they need, and they can't figure out what it is.

We have an extraordinary task - to pass on the Message that our Father is real, that His Word has strength and can change lives.

Sometimes being a soldier of God is not easy, but everything that is done in the name of God is possible to achieve. The reward at the end of the road will be the Glory of God in all its splendor.

Jehovah has promised us eternal life. Let's be the ones to keep His

Word. Let us take the message to many people so that they may know the true life in Christ.

Let's make the difference between living in a world without hope or living with God on our behalf and witnessing the miracle of life.

Mirian Cukovic

Record your Notes or Reflections:

When was the last time you made a difference in someone's life?
What did you do?
How can you make a difference in the lives of others?

_____

_____

_____

_____

_____

_____

_____

_____

_____

God's Plan

"Then God said, 'Let us make man in our image, after our likeness. And let them have dominion over the fish of the sea and over the birds of the heavens and over the livestock and over all the earth and over every creeping thing that creeps on the earth.'" - Genesis 1:26, English Standard Version

God's original plan was to be one with us in the garden of Eden. That is still God's plan for each and every one of us. We were created in His image. He loves us deeply with a steadfast love.

Not only that, but we were created in His likeness. God created us to be just like Him, living a life of perfect harmony with the trinity and without sin, understanding and operating in unconditional love for one another.

Don't let social distancing become isolation. We all need each other to survive. Your gifts and talents are needed to build up the kingdom of God. We are much stronger and more effective when we work together. He chose me, you, us, to share in His inheritance.

We must constantly remind ourselves that no matter what is going on around us, we are still loved and protected by God. When times seem dark, look to the light of the world. That light is Jesus Christ. God's plan will never fail and neither will His love for you and I. It has always been in His plan to have unity and community amongst the family of believers.

Veniss Aguilerra

Record your Notes or Reflections:

Knowing that you are created in His image and in His likeness, where do you see yourself in His plan during this season of your life?

_____

_____

_____

_____

_____

_____

_____

_____

_____

_____

_____

_____

_____

_____

_____

_____

_____

_____

_____

_____

_____

_____

_____

_____

_____

_____

_____

_____

_____

Faith in God

"Now faith is the assurance of things hoped for, the conviction of things not seen." - Hebrews 11:1, English Standard Version

Father, I pray that the message You have given me is made clear to others. I pray for anyone who wants to trust You to know that the way to do it is to trust that Your word is true. I pray that You work on the hearts that want to know You; help us to trust You. In the name of Jesus, Amen.

Faith is a gift from God. The question is not how do I obtain faith, but how to apply the faith that is in me to my everyday circumstance. We all have faith in something. We have faith in our ability to drive our car, or faith in a person we trust. Where we need to focus our faith exclusively is on the living God, on Jesus Christ. Faith comes from hearing the word of God. Faith is being sure of what we expect, what we hope for, and what we see. Faith involves believing first and then seeing. God called Abraham "Father of many nations." The Bible tells us that Abraham believed that this promise would be fulfilled. He did not wait until he saw the physical evidence before believing by faith. But eventually, he saw it with his own eyes.

God honors your faith every day and God is honoring your faith today. You will see the Lord keep his promises! Continue using the measure of faith that God has given you.

Vilma Tricoche

Record your Notes or Reflections:

When going through difficult times, where is your faith?

_____

_____

_____

_____

_____

_____

_____

_____

_____

_____

_____

_____

_____

_____

_____

We Have Power Through Jesus

"Behold, I give you the authority to trample on serpents and scorpions, and over all the power of the enemy, and nothing shall by any means hurt you." - Luke 10:19, New King James Version

We have power because Jesus has given it to us. Just as people eat healthy food, maintain a rhythm of exercises, and lift weights to have strong muscles, so must we be diligent for our spiritual strength.

Reading the Holy Scriptures helps us to acquire knowledge, as well as learn about the promises, the plan of God, and the most important things that will train us for the difficult situations and circumstances in our lives. We have to learn the Word of God because it has power.

Praise and worship help our spiritual power because they magnify God; we don't focus on ourselves during worship, but on God. Through praise, our joy increases, and our emotions rise. Fear, worry, and doubt cannot survive in an atmosphere of praise.

Our Power also increases with prayer because we are talking to God. He will communicate and guide us through our paths. When we pray, we open our hearts to God to tell Him about the things that happen in our lives, and our relationship with Him is strengthened. All solutions and answers can come through contact with Almighty God.

We have power when we call on the name of Jesus because we have everything that Jesus has and everything that He has earned.

For this reason, "…God also has highly exalted Him and given Him the name which is above every name, that at the name of Jesus every knee should bow, of those in heaven, and of those on earth, and of those under the earth." (Philippians 2: 9-10, New King James Version)

When we read the Holy Scriptures, pray, praise, worship, and mention the name of Jesus, we have power to face the obstacles of this life.

Ingrid Quevedo

Record your Notes or Reflections:
What are the means that you are using to obtain the power that God has for you?

_____

_____

_____

_____

_____

_____

_____

_____

God is Near

"Come near to God and He will come near to you...." - James 4:8a, New International Version

God is nearer than we think. Many may imagine God to be in the heavens very far away from us, but according to the Bible, if we come near to God, He will come near to us. Why do we need to make the first move? Because God has given us free will, and He will never force His will upon us.

If we look at the parable of the Prodigal Son, we see a father who represents God, and the lost son as all of us who were lost. The son, after abandoning his family and squandering his inheritance, realizes his mistakes and decides to go back to his father. As he starts his trek back home, the scripture says that while the son was still a long way off, his father saw him and *ran* over to receive him back.

This is a wonderful example of how our heavenly Father is watching and waiting for us to start to come near to Him, to accept Him. Once we make that first move, He runs to us to give us His love, His compassion, His mercy, His forgiveness.

We need to be thankful that God honors our decisions and when we decide to come near to Him, He is more than willing to come closer and nearer to us, accept us, and embrace us into His family. Come near to God starting today.

Jonathan Quevedo

Record your Notes or Reflections:

What comfort do you find when you realize that God is looking to come near to you if you let Him?

_____

_____

_____

_____

_____

_____

_____

_____

_____

_____

_____

_____

_____

Answer God's Call

"...and in the wilderness. There you saw how the Lord your God carried you, as a father carries his son, all the way you went until you reached this place." - Deuteronomy 1:31, New International Version

Many times, you wonder where God is and if He can hear your cry. God is constantly speaking to you, but are you listening? Do you hear God calling you? There is a reason for your existence that was planned before conception. What is God saying to you? Are you ready to answer His call? God is calling you to live purposefully, to live beyond expectations.

Do not minimize God's calling. Do not let fear hold you back from what has been ordained for your life. It won't be easy; nothing worth it is easy. There is a reason you went through the pain, the brokenness, the rejection, the loneliness, the hurt. There is a reason you felt alone; however, God was with you the entire time and He carried you through it all. The recovery is more painful than the thing that broke you, but He is ready to mend the broken pieces in your life so that He can complete the work He started in you.

Don't expect people to cheer you on in your battle. Some may laugh and mock you, but your obedience will be the very thing that will help you persevere. When you see the grace and mercy that God is going to show you, you will have your story. Your story that you will share with others, the story that will be the reason why you will attract a new tribe. The enemy will be under your feet and you will dance, praise, and shout to the King.

Keila Vera

Record your Notes or Reflections:
Can you hear what God is trying to tell you?
What is God calling you to do?
What is stopping you from being obedient?
Write a personal prayer to move forward.

_____

_____

_____

_____

_____

_____

_____

_____

_____

I Am A Light

"You are the light of the world. A town built on a hill cannot be hidden. Neither do people light a lamp and put it under a bowl. Instead they put it on its stand, and it gives light to everyone in the house. In the same way, let your light shine before others, that they may see your good deeds and glorify your Father in heaven." - New International Version, Matthew 5:14-16

There is a host of star-shaped glow-in-the-dark stickers on my bedroom ceiling. Before drifting to sleep, I gaze at the twinkling lights making a combination of constellations and special designs that my son creatively applied. Of all the glow star designs above me, there is one that stands out - my shortened name - *Charl*. I realize that this subtle configuration is more than the artistic inner workings of a gifted artist. It was what this young man saw through me. I am not sure if he would see discipline as a good deed. In this constellation of lights, God reminds me of who He called me to be. It is who I am: a light. The world is darkened by fear, greed, hurt, a lack of forgiveness. Many walk around with a dull hue of existing. while others carry a dimly lit measure of hope.

But, I (and you) have a light dwelling within that illuminates the path to living. All we need to do is to *shine*! Did you know that you may be the nearest sparkle of God that someone is praying for? But how? Let your light shine through words of encouragement, comfort, and wisdom. Paul's letter to the Philippians reminds us to think upon that which is excellent or praiseworthy. In other words, let your light shine by choosing to focus on the positive. Negativity is like pouring water on a flame - its glow is quickly extinguished.

Let your light shine through kind, good acts towards others. You do not know whose darkened days will be made brighter through your going out of your way to be a helping hand, a shoulder to lean on, or even an ear that listens. He is always with you and will never leave you. Let your light shine.

Charlotte Diakite

Record your Notes or Reflections:
Where and how will you be a light today?

_____

_____

_____

_____

_____

_____

_____

_____

Trust God and the Process

"My fellow believers, when it seems as though you are facing nothing but difficulties see it as an invaluable opportunity to experience the greatest joy that you can! For you know that when your faith is tested it stirs up power within you to endure all things. And then as your endurance grows even stronger it will release perfection into every part of your being until there is nothing missing and nothing lacking." James 1:2-4, The Passion Translation

I struggled with trust and noticed it stumped my spiritual journey. One day, I heard, "Candi, it is hard to trust the process if you can't trust ME." God was loud and clear, and I finally got it!

Allow me to share: when people disappoint and hurt you, it is part of the process, your journey. When they speak ill of you and turn their back on you, it is part of the process. When you are smiling and offering your hand to help, and they stab you in the back, it is part of the process. When you trust with all your heart and someone rips your heart out and stomps on it, it is part of the process.

God allows these things to happen to shape and mold us, build up our character, and rid us of things that are not of Him that we don't realize exist in us or around us. Some of the molding He allows can be very uncomfortable, but we have to trust God and the process. God is at work to perfect the best creation of us; purpose must be birthed and activated.

While trusting the process, be courageous – allow yourself to take risks; set boundaries – get in alignment with God's will for your life; learn the lesson – see failures as lessons and not losses; and sharpen your discernment and be obedient – know when it is God and obey His directive.

Remember, "And we know that all things work together for good to those who love God, to those who are called according to His purpose." (Romans 8:28) "If God is for you, then who can be against you?" (Romans 8:31)

Candi Young

Record your Notes or Reflections:
What do you need to do today to trust God and the process of your life?

_____

_____

_____

_____

_____

_____

_____

Soul Security

"I have set the Lord always before me; because he is at my right hand, I shall not be moved." - Psalms 16:8, King James Version

We want financial security. We want secure homes, secure positions with our employers, secure marriages, and secure friendships. When we go into establishments like a restaurant, a shopping mall, movie theater, or skating rink, we expect to feel secure. It is human nature to want to protect who and what you love and to also feel protected. When we lack security, fear sneaks in, along with its partners - anxiety and paranoia.

No matter how many security cameras and alarm systems we have, God is our first and ultimate line of defense in all that we want to protect. We go to great lengths to protect our homes, pay hefty amounts for insurance premiums, jump in front of a speeding train to save our children, but what are we doing to protect our souls?

I pray that every single day of our life, we are seeking God. We study His word, follow His commandments, share the good news, acknowledge Him in all our ways, and delight ourselves in Him so that He may direct our path. We do just what the psalmist said - to set the Lord before us because when He is at our right hand, we cannot be moved. That, my friend, is soul security! Hallelujah!

Veniss Aguilerra

Record your Notes or Reflections:

In what ways are you securing your soul to be sure you spend eternity with our Lord and Savior, Jesus Christ?

You are Special

"For you created my inmost being; you knit me together in my mother's womb. I praise you because I am fearfully and wonderfully made; your works are wonderful, I know that full well." - Psalm 139: 13-14, New International Version

God is a Creator who is never without inspiration. Each of His creations is unique, and so are we.

God tells us, "You are my Masterpiece." In us, God has put spiritual gifts, natural abilities, character and personality, knowledge and experiences, and the relationships that we have developed into our lives. He wants us to use them. We have great value because of what our Heavenly Father says about us and what He has done for each of us.

Psalm 139 declares every detail of each of our lives, not only examining the miraculous gift of the human body, but also the majesty of our Heavenly Father's love for humanity. Our stature, figure, and structures were designed by God. He made us exactly the way He wanted us to, and it all started before we were born. God has a special purpose for each person who is born. We are not an accident, nor do we exist by chance. God formed us many, many years ago before we took our first breath.

We have unique qualities that God will use to accomplish His purpose, and He wants us to be successful.

God wants us to love ourselves, not with pride, but in a way that we truly understand how special we are to Him. When we begin to look at ourselves, how God sees us, then we can love ourselves.

God loves us and appreciated us long before we were conceived by our parents, because He had already conceived us in His mind.

We are who we are for a reason.

We are part of a detailed plan.

We are unique creatures, beautifully designed.

Let's never let someone's opinion of us interrupt God's call for our life.

Ingrid Quevedo

Record your Notes or Reflections:

How does it make you feel, knowing that you are special?

_____

_____

_____

_____

_____

_____

Persevere

"Blessed is the one who perseveres under trial because, having stood the test, that person will receive the crown of life that the Lord has promised to those who love him." - New International Version, James 1:12

When I opened my construction company, which was supposed to lead me up mountains of happiness, I at times found myself struggling out of valleys of trials and tests. Here I was, leading a company in an industry I knew absolutely nothing about. But my husband was a working carpenter striving for business ownership. After a twelve-year productive corporate career, I was released, suddenly unemployed and at the crossroad. Together with my husband, I took a faith step towards a family-owned business.

One day, I found myself deep in a faith-test valley. From skyline-views of the corporate office to the nails and hammers of a construction site, I felt like a fish out of water. I don't understand blueprints or roofing slopes. What am I doing here? I should just return to what I know: marketing and spreadsheets. That same day, I took a drive, ending at a bayside marina. The water was so still. Looking across the bay, tears formed. I closed my eyes, perhaps to stop seeing failure. Or did I close my eyes to imagine hope and prosperity? I called out, "Lord, please, what am I to do?"

After a while, my eyes blinked to refocus on a large sight. There in the bay was a slow-moving large-sized ship. On the front and back sides were big white-colored letters: PERSEVERE. I followed, with a locked gaze, the slow movement of this imposing figure. Time stood still. I heard and felt God. It was clear to me that God is bigger than these trials and tests.

There emerged a new strength and faith that lifted me out of the valley. From that day on, I stuck it out as the owner of a blessed, fruitful company. Circumstances and challenges sometimes bring me to the trial-test valley. Now, with closed eyes, I thank God for that large-lettered ship in the bay.

Charlotte Diakite

Record your Notes or Reflections:
For each letter, share your own word, expression or scripture that can encourage you to: P. E. R. S. E.V. E. R. E.

_____

_____

_____

_____

_____

_____

_____

_____

Immediate Obedience

"When He had stopped speaking, He said to Simon, 'Launch out into the deep and let down your nets for a catch.' But Simon answered and said to Him, 'Master, we have toiled all night and caught nothing; nevertheless at Your word I will let down the net.' And when they had done this, they caught a great number of fish, and their net was breaking. So they signaled to their partners in the other boat to come and help them. And they came and filled both the boats, so that they began to sink." Luke 5:4-7, New King James Version

Simon Peter thought Jesus's directive made absolutely no sense, yet he obeyed anyway. Take note of the timing of Peter's obedience - it was immediate, and the results were an abundant reward. Our immediate obedience is important.

The first time the Lord told me to leave my corporate job after a 24-year tenure, I immediately dismissed it as the voice of the enemy. Why would God tell me to leave my job with no retirement package while my eldest son was about to pursue higher education? It made no sense.

Within a year, the voice of the Lord came to me again, and again, I dismissed it as the voice of the enemy. This time, there was more at stake. In my disobedience, I lost a lot through job stress that attacked my physical and mental health.

Three years later, the voice of the Lord came to me yet again, but this time, I immediately sought God and obeyed. My immediate obedience brought restoration physically, mentally, emotionally, and spiritually… priceless.

In my freedom, I came to understand who I am and whose I am. There have been challenging times, especially during the 2020 COVID-19 pandemic, but GOD kept me. That saying is not a cliché.

We need to recognize what hinders our immediate obedience and fight against it - lack of faith with fear of the unknown, lack of trust and total surrender to God, and lack of understanding God's Will for our lives.

Proverbs 3:5-6 states, "Trust in the Lord with all your heart, And lean not on your own understanding; In all your ways acknowledge Him, And He shall direct your paths." Seek God and get in alignment with His Word and Will for your life; you will find the strength and faith within to respond with immediate obedience.

Candi Young

Record your Notes or Reflections:
Are you clear between the Lord's voice, your voice, and the enemy's voice?
What stops you from immediate obedience to the voice of God?

_____

_____

_____

Declaration and Praise of Thanksgiving

"Lord! I'm bursting with joy over what you have done for me! My lips are full of perpetual praise. I'm boasting of you and all your works, so let all who are discouraged take heart. Listen to my testimony: I cried to God in my distress and He answered me. He freed me from all my fears! I cried out to the Lord and He heard me, bringing this miracle - deliverance when I needed it most." - Psalm 34:1-2, 4, 6, The Passion Translation

For many people, a positive COVID-19 test result was a death sentence or at minimum, a very fearful and harrowing experience. On October 16, 2020, I tested positive. Upon reviewing the results, my heart started beating faster, and my thoughts were all over the place. What does this mean? What am I going to do? I felt fear and guilt gripping at my heart. What if I had compromised my family's health?

I took a deep breath, composed myself, and prayed. I asked God to take control, to bring healing, and give me peace. I experienced a lot of different emotions and began to declare Psalms 118:17 over my life, "I shall not die, but live, and declare the works of the Lord." God is faithful! He heard and answered my prayers. Not one of my family members tested positive at the time. Not my grandchildren and especially not my 80-year-old mother, who I continued to care for during quarantine. I made my own the promises declared in Psalm 34. I encourage you to look to God in all situations and circumstances. What the enemy of our soul may devise for our death, God will turn it around and redeem it for life. Hallelujah!

Lord, I thank You for your goodness and mercies. What You have done for me, You will do for others too. May there be a perpetual praise in my heart and on my lips for who You are and what You have done. Amen.

Maria Rivera

Record your Notes or Reflections:
Write down praises of blessings and thanksgiving to remember in times of discouragement. Write declarations over your life.

_____

_____

_____

_____

_____

_____

_____

_____

Chosen, not Trapped

"And we know that for those who love God all things work together for good, for those who are called according to his purpose." - Romans 8:28, English Standard Version

And just like that, everything changed. A few months of caring for my husband turned into something I could have never imagined and wouldn't have wished on my worst enemy.

I became a caregiver to my husband July 2019 as a result of serious diabetes-related complications and was filled with anger and bitterness. This was his fault and wouldn't have happened if he had just taken his medication, and I had no problem telling him so. He was once a big strapping man but now required total care. I was caring for him alright, but my heart was tarnished. I wasn't only upset with him; I was upset with God. I felt trapped and I had no problem telling God either.

Though things were difficult, and his needs steadily increased, I found myself completing his "nursing" tasks with ease. My children were amazed with my newfound wound care expertise and commended my efforts, but all I could focus on were the things I wasn't able to do because of his illness.

Then God dealt with me. I can't say I heard an audible voice, but my spirit said, "You aren't trapped - you were chosen." He said this journey was mine and had nothing to do with my husband. And just like that, my heart was softened and I accepted my assignment. I was supposed to be instrumental in his physical healing while God healed me. I took leave from my job to genuinely care for him and create an environment where God's healing glory could flourish.

When God chooses you, there is no opportunity for failure. When you are functioning in the purposes of God, every trial, all things really do work for the good of the Kingdom.

No matter the assignment, it will work out for good because God is a good God. Take some time and check your heart. God can't fail and He chose you!

Joyce Travers-Johnson

Record your Notes or Reflections:
Has there been a time when you knew God chose you for an assignment and you weren't fully on board?
A time where your assignment was a task and not a labor of love unto God?

_____

_____

_____

_____

_____

_____

My Body, God's Temple

"Do you not know that your bodies are temples of the Holy Spirit, who is in you, whom you have received from God? You are not your own." - 1 Corinthians 6:19, New International Version

We were chosen as children of God, so our bodies became the temple where our Father dwells.

How do we take care of our bodies? Do we keep our bodies clean of all worldly impurity for God? What does God want us to do with our bodies? Always obsessed with fashion, new lifestyles, and Hollywood movie stars who force us to compete with them? As a result of this lifestyle and these starlets, we do not accept ourselves and want to change constantly. In many cases, this has reached extreme circumstances to achieve the goals that society has imposed, especially on teenagers and young adults.

Social media is affecting us rapidly, and not just showing us people working in the media, but also friends and family from around the world, making it even harder to not to be part of it.

Our body is God's masterpiece. He believes us in His image and likeness; therefore, we are fortunate beings to be part of this wonder of God.

Jehovah loves us as we are. We are His children and as such, we must accept ourselves with our skills or with our limitations. We are what

God wants us to be, because for Him, everything has a purpose. Let us not focus on our limitations, but rather our virtues. Let us be the example of life that God wants us to be. Let's get the best out of us and show it to the world. We are His creation and we are worthy to have it in our hearts, in our minds, and spirit.

Let's say to the whole world here - I am and I love myself just the way God loves me, and I want to consecrate my body to you, Father, as your dwelling.

Mirian Cukovic

Record your Notes or Reflections:

What do you see when you step in front of the mirror?

Do you see yourself as God's perfect creation?

Where are you struggling with acceptance?

_____

_____

_____

_____

_____

_____

_____

Who is Jesus?

"Go therefore, go and make disciples of all nations, baptizing them in the name of the Father, and of the Son, and of the Holy Spirit, teaching them to observe all things that I have commanded you; and Io, I am with you always, even to the end of the age." - Matthew 28:19-20, New King James Version

Who is Jesus? What do we do once we know Him? How do we take what we've learned and apply it to our lives? Some will choose to ignore the Good News, but the truth is that we only have two options. We can accept Jesus as our Lord and Savior, or we can choose to ignore Him. How exactly do we accept Jesus in our life? We have to believe in Him. This means having confidence in God, knowing that His death on Calvary and on the cross paid for all our sins. This is not simply an intellectual understanding; on the contrary, it is to submit ourselves totally to Jesus as the only one who can forgive our sins, thus forming a bridge and serving as a gap between us and our Father.

When we receive Jesus as our Savior, we immediately become the children of the King. As believers, we have to follow in the footsteps of Jesus, allowing Him to have control in our lives. We have to be flexible so that our desires are in Him. In addition, as Christians and followers of Jesus, we have to worship Him. We must be so moved by His presence that our hearts and lips overflow with adoration. Finally, we have to share the truth with others. Before Jesus ascended into heaven, He called His followers so that they could carry the message of salvation to the whole world. We are very blessed with having access to the word of God. Once we know who He is, we must declare with enthusiasm that He is Lord of our lives. Jesus wants to have a long personal intimate relationship with you.

Vilma Tricoche

Record your Notes or Reflections:

Do you want to say yes to Jesus's offer?
What can you personally do to carry out the great commission found in Matthew 28:19?

_____

_____

_____

_____

_____

_____

_____

_____

_____

Total Surrender

"Therefore, I urge you, brothers and sisters, in view of God's mercy, to offer your bodies as a living sacrifice, holy and pleasing to God–this is your true worship. Do not conform to the pattern of this world but be transformed by the renewing of your mind. Then you will be able to test and approve what God's will is – his good, pleasing and perfect will." - Romans 12:1-2, New International Version

If you want a change in your life, if you want forgiveness and peace and joy that you have never experienced before, God demands total surrender. He is the ruler of your life. When you fly in a plane, you surrender to the plane. The plane is carrying you and your belongings. When you are in surgery, you surrender to the doctors who will use medication to put you to sleep and the instruments to cut you. You need to realize that you cannot do it on your own, and you were not created to live life alone.

Lean on Him for wisdom and understanding. Surrender your mind, how you think and what you think. Don't let the devil corrupt your mind. The more idle time you have, the more he tries to corrupt your way of thinking. Keep your eyes fixed on God. Surrender your body. The bible says if you are a Christian, your body does not belong to you - it belongs to God. Your body is God's temple and He dwells in you when you have a relationship with Him. You have the opportunity to start a new life; He will forgive all of your past and give you power for the future. Your heart can be changed through prayer, reading the bible, and listening to the Holy Spirit. Surrender your will. He knows what you need, He knows your battles, He knows your struggles. He wants you to proclaim it from your mouth: "Lord, I will receive you into my heart. Forgive me of my past and the things I have done wrong. Give me a new direction in my life." It is changed by surrender.

Keila Vera

Record your Notes or Reflections:

Write all that you need to surrender to God. "Lord, today, I surrender…"

_____

_____

_____

_____

_____

_____

_____

_____

_____

He Who Watches Us

"From heaven the Lord looks down and sees all mankind; from his dwelling place he watches all who live on earth." - Psalm 33:13-14, New International Version

Psalm 33 should give us some reassurance that we are watched over. As a result, we should feel safe and secure.

As a good parent, you watch over your child and try to provide, guide, shelter, and protect them to the best of your ability. And as a parent, you are attentive when they cry out for your help. How much more would that apply to our Great Heavenly Father with us?

We see this idea in Matthew 7:9-11 - "Which of you, if your son asks for bread, will give him a stone? Or if he asks for a fish, will give him a snake? If you, then though you are evil, know how to give good gifts to your children, how much more will your Father who is in heaven give good things to those who ask Him!" Even though we may try our best as parents, when we are compared to the Holy and perfect nature of God, we fall short and are considered evil.

As we journey through life, in this imperfect, fallen world, we know that we will face trials and hardships, but we know that whatever we face, we are watched over by a loving God who will see us through. God has said that he will never leave us or forsake us.

Our heavenly Father is constantly looking out for us. We must be alert and discern what it is He has to say. We must realize that we can never escape or hide from His observations, and we must be alert to His watchful eye and instructions, because He watches over us.

Jonathan Quevedo

Record your Notes or Reflections:
Does knowing that God is always watching give you comfort or concern?
Express how and why.

_____

_____

_____

_____

_____

_____

_____

_____

Loved One Lost

"Suppose one of you has a hundred sheep and loses one of them. Doesn't he leave the ninety-nine in the open country and go after the lost sheep until he finds it? I tell you that in the same way there will be more rejoicing in heaven over one sinner who repents than over ninety-nine righteous persons who do not need to repent."- New International Version, Luke 15:4, 7

Here is a prayer for someone you know who is searching for God.

Lord Jesus, the Good Shepherd. Your Word proclaims that You will leave the 99 sheep and go to search for the one that is lost. You said that You would lay down Your life for Your sheep. You left others who followed You to find the man possessed, the woman at the well, the tax collector, and many more.

Right now, there is one who is lost. I bring to the foot of Your throne my loved one lost, (*name*). I stand in the gap for loved one lost, (*name*). I rebuke the spirit of rebellion against You, in Jesus' name. I raise a cry for deliverance, grace, and mercy. Loved one lost, (*name*), is searching for truth. You are the Way, the Truth, and the Life. Loved one, (*name*), wants to know You. Your sheep know Your voice. Loved one (*name*) seeks peace. You leave us peace, not as the world gives, but Your perfect peace that surpasses all understanding.

Loved one (*name*) feels hopeless and without joy. You are the anchor of hope. Loved one (*name*) rejects Your authority and sovereignty.

You are the Creator of all things and the Sustainer of everything. You are the Great I AM. Loved one (*name*) feels unloved and unworthy. Lord, You are love. Loved one lost (*name*) wants to be saved, but does not know how. Please Lord, touch (*his/her*) heart to humbly repent and surrender to You. Find (*him/her*), Lord. And when loved one lost (*name*) is found, may it be like the return of the prodigal son coming home to his rejoicing father with wondrous praise heard high in the heavens and below on earth, for loved one lost (*name*) will find eternal life with You.

Hallelujah. Amen.

Charlotte Diakite

Record your Notes or Reflections:
Write the names of the loved ones you are praying for.

_____

_____

_____

_____

_____

_____

_____

Faith is All You Need

"Now faith brings hopes into reality and becomes the foundation needed to acquire the things we long for. It is all the evidence required to prove what is still unseen." - Hebrews 11:1, The Passion Translation

Hope is the feeling that what you want can be had or that events will turn out for the best. You hope that your favorite team will win a tournament. You hope your crush will ask you out. You hope that it doesn't rain while on vacation. You hope your cancer treatments are successful. You hope you can get through a difficult situation.

Do you have faith in the God you serve? Unlike hope, faith can move mountains. All you need is faith as small as a mustard seed. God is waiting for you and will meet you right where you are. Everything you have ever hoped for is yours when you have faith. When God sees the effort that you make to love Him, believe in Him, accept Him as your Lord and Savior, He will provide what you need at the time you need it and at His time He sees fit. God's timing is always perfect. He will never leave you, nor forsake you; do not be discouraged.

You were destined for greatness; it was written before you were born and God will see to it that you, His child, acquire the inheritance promised to you. Spending time with God will strengthen your faith and build on your relationship with Him. As you build your personal relationship with Him, He will get to know more of you and you will get to know more of Him. I encourage you to pray daily, read your bible, read a devotional. Through this, your strengthened faith will bring your hopes into reality.

Keila Vera

Record your Notes or Reflections:
What steps can you take to strengthen your faith?

_____

_____

_____

_____

_____

_____

_____

_____

_____

_____

_____

Forgiveness

"And forgive us our debts, as we forgive our debtors." "For if ye forgive men their trespasses, your heavenly Father will also forgive you: But if ye forgive not men their trespasses, neither will your Father forgive your trespasses." - Matthew 6:12, 14-15, King James Version

Forgiveness is excusing another for an action considered an offense, renouncing

possible revenge, and choosing to disregard the offense in the future, so that relationships will be restored.

There are unexpected events that take place in life that cause heartache, offenses, and if not addressed speedily, allow for a lifetime of grief. Without going into details, there was an unprecedented event that occurred in my immediate family. My extended family were notified of the incident and they became involved. Words were spoken and decisions were made in anger that could have had detrimental consequences in my immediate family. This weighed heavily on my heart and I allowed myself to feel offended.

As the days passed, I realized that harboring these feelings in my heart was not right before God. I had to repent and forgive, especially if I wanted my faults before God to be forgiven. Yet I wanted to do it my way. I was going to forgive, but I wanted the person who offended me to know how much I was hurt.

I had to allow God to heal my heart. As I prayed and went to God about it, I meditated on all that Jesus Christ, the Son of God, had to endure on the cross of Calvary. It puts that offense that you keep holding onto in your heart into perspective about how small and insignificant it really is.

I heard clearly in my heart, "When you ask Me for forgiveness, do I forgive you?" Yes, Lord. You forgive me. "Do I say, I forgive you, but let Me tell you how you hurt Me?" No, Lord. You simply forgive me and forget my offenses.

It was then that I understood I had to forgive as He forgives without opening my mouth to say what I felt or thought, to restore the relationship. I prayed to God and asked Him to help me forgive as He did. By God's grace and mercy, there was sincere forgiveness and restoration.

Lord, make me a vessel of forgiveness, an instrument of Your love and kindness.

Maria Rivera

Record your Notes or Reflections:

In order to be forgiven, we have to be quick to release forgiveness.
Who do you have to forgive today?
What relationships need to be restored?

_____

_____

_____

Rejoice in the Lord

"Rejoice in the Lord always. Again I will say, rejoice!" - Philippians 4:4, English Standard Version

What a joy it is to be in the presence of the Lord! I am rejoicing!

I am rejoicing because the world told me that I am not good enough, but God said, "Yes, you are. You were made in My image. I have a plan for you."

I am rejoicing because I have victory in Christ.

I am rejoicing because my sins have been forgiven through the blood of Jesus.

I am rejoicing because I have power and authority through my Lord Jesus.

I am rejoicing because I am healed. Even if an illness takes my life, it can't take my spirit, because I belong to God.

I am rejoicing because my trials are coming back-to-back. But I count it all as joy. I am equipped with the whole armor of God. My troubles won't last always.

I am rejoicing because I have strength in the Lord. When I'm weak, He is strong; when my heart is broken, He is close to me.

I am rejoicing because I can do all things through Christ.

I am rejoicing because God has granted me knowledge and understanding of His Holy Word. Without it, where would we be? The truth has set us free.

I am rejoicing because it makes the enemy mad. He thought he had me, but I rest in the shelter of the wing of The Most High God.

I am rejoicing because God is my provider and He meets all my needs. The Lord is my Shepherd; I shall not want.

Veniss Aguilerra

Record your Notes or Reflections:
In what ways do you feel the joy of God in your life?
What makes you happy about your relationship with Him?

_____

_____

_____

_____

_____

_____

_____

_____

Wait on the Lord

"But those who wait for the Lord will gain new strength and renew their power; they will lift up their wings like eagles; they will run and not become weary, they will walk and not grow tired." - Isaiah 40:31, Amplified Bible

Many times, we want to do things our way and get results right away, but life is not like that. If we trust and hope in the Lord, we will see results.

Things happen because the Lord wants them to happen, and sometimes, He causes delays for us to get closer to Him. But everything that happens is not a mistake.

The Lord has our whole life programmed, although, sometimes, we deviate from God's plan. I got married when I was twenty years old, and became a widow a short three years later at the age of twenty-three with a three-year-old son. I wanted a better future for my child, and chose to come from my home country of Honduras to the United States. I had to leave my baby boy with my sister since I could only obtain a visa for myself. I lived with my other sister in the United States, and waited five years to obtain my permanent residency. I was unable to see my son for five years! It was the most difficult time of my life, but I did it with faith in the Lord.

When we know and trust the promises of God, it is wonderful. The process is not easy, but you have to trust and be patient, because it is not our time but God's time. He always works for our well-being. Since coming to the United States, my son graduated from New Jersey Institute of Technology and is an engineer, so we thank our God because without Him, we are nobody and with Him, we are everything.

Vilma Tricoche

Record your Notes or Reflections:
When times are rough, do not give up. Wait on the Lord. What are you waiting on?

_____

_____

_____

_____

_____

_____

_____

_____

_____

Let Us Pray

"Now this is the confidence that we have in Him, that if we ask anything according to His will, He hears us. And if we know that He hears us, whatever we ask, we know that we have the petitions that we have asked of Him." - 1 John 5:14-15, New King James Version

Father God, in the mighty name of Jesus, this is the day that You have made; we shall rejoice and be glad in it. Father, thank You for another day filled with Your loving kindness and mercy. You are a magnificent God, and we want to be called Your friend. Lord, help us to seek and strengthen our relationship with You. We trust and acknowledge You in all of our ways so You can direct our paths into peace and spiritual prosperity. No matter what the situation looks like, we have faith that You are already working it out. Thank You for making us the head and not the tail, above and not beneath, more than conquerors in all things. Thank You for 100% victory 100% of the time.

Hallelujah! We cry out for the children, Abba. Help them make sound decisions, as they daily seek Your guidance. May they love and respect their parents. Heal those who have been hurt and scarred so they no longer hurt themselves or others. Help them to forgive and have love in their hearts. Lord, help us to raise this generation to love, respect, honor, and be like You; living and walking in God's Will for their lives. Holy Spirit, teach them to pray and to clearly hear and receive Your guidance and direction. We pray this generation will turn back to You, Lord. Move us to humble ourselves, repent, and seek You. Change hearts and minds to feel and think as You. Strengthen and prepare future generations to worship and honor You. Bless us, Lord, as we plead the blood of Jesus over our lives. In the mighty name of Jesus, we lift up this prayer. Amen!

Candi Young

Record your Notes or Reflections:

Have you meditated and asked God's will for your life?

What do you need to take to God through prayer?

_____

_____

_____

_____

_____

_____

_____

_____

Beyond the Surface

"Do not judge by appearance {superficially and arrogantly} but judge fairly and righteously." - John 7:24, Amplified Bible

Although we've all heard the saying *Don't judge a book by its cover*, I'm sure many have done just that. We've assumed a person was well-to-do because they lived in a certain area, attended certain schools, or drove a particular car. We tend to size each other up during awkward introductions, all the while forming unfair and probably inaccurate opinions of one another. What if we're wrong? What if the popular cheerleader is just as insecure as you, and conversely, if the shy kid is a piano virtuoso in the making? What if we thought about the times people might have formed opinions about us that didn't reflect our true character? What if we decided to look beyond the surface?

Take a journey with me for a minute. During the COVID-19 pandemic, I decided to switch out some of the shrubs in front of my house. Though they were green, their growth appeared to be stunted and they never grew beyond two feet, unlike the four-to-five feet promised by the salesperson.

I previously laid mulch to minimize the possibility of weeds from forming. As I removed the mulch and started to dig, I was met with a web of resistance. Just beneath the surface, I found a system of roots from mint that was planted years ago that literally spanned the length of the entire bed. The roots were intertwined and robust, almost seeming intentional in their architecture.

The mint, planted to help ward off insects, had taken over just beneath the surface. The elaborate root system prevented the other plants from thriving. At a glance, the bed looked beautiful, but just beneath the surface, something that was once helpful had now become detrimental and prevented the entire bed from thriving.

This reminds me of our relationship with Christ. Are we surface Christians, never taking the time to "dig deeper" into the word? Do we stop at the surface and avoid getting to the root so we can weed out the things that are stunting our growth? God has plans to prosper us, but we won't walk into our full purpose if we don't go beyond a surface relationship with our savior.

Joyce Travers-Johnson

Record your Notes or Reflections:
What's standing in your way of growth?

_____

_____

_____

_____

_____

_____

Beyond the Storm Clouds

"I leave the gift of peace with you-my peace. Not the kind of fragile peace given by the world, but my perfect peace. Don't yield to fear or be troubled in your hearts-instead be courageous!" - John 14:27, The Passion Translation

When there is a storm raging around us, what do we notice and dwell on? Usually, we see the pouring rain, the dark, threatening clouds, and the frightening lightning. We do not realize that beyond the storm clouds, the sun is still shining. The sun does not disappear during a thunderstorm. The sun and the bright shining skies are only beyond the storm clouds.

When you are faced with a difficult situation, do you tend to focus and think about the circumstances that surround you? We tend to see only the problem, but often do not look beyond the situation.

In the Bible, a similar problem existed with the apostle Peter, when the disciples were in a boat and Jesus came walking on the water to them. The boat was being tossed about by high winds and heavy seas from a fierce storm, but Jesus told them not to be afraid. Peter said that if it was really Jesus, He should call him out onto the water. So, Jesus called Peter. Peter stepped out and began to walk to Jesus, but when he realized how high the waves were, he became frightened and started to sink. Jesus saved him before he drowned. Peter wasn't frightened when he first stepped onto the water, only because he was focused on Jesus. Once he took his eyes off Jesus and looked at the waves, Peter's troubles truly began.

We must keep our eyes fixed on Jesus, no matter what the situation or circumstance. The Son of God is shining beyond our problematic storm clouds. May God give us the ability to always acknowledge Him above and see beyond every situation that we face.

Jonathan Quevedo

Record your Notes or Reflections:
What storm clouds are you needing to look beyond?

_____

_____

_____

_____

_____

_____

_____

_____

Promise to Worship

"But a time is coming, and even now has arrived, when the true worshipers will worship the Father in spirit and truth; for such people the Father seeks to be His worshipers. God is spirit, and those who worship Him must worship in spirit and truth." - John 4:23-24, New American Standard Version

The Bible is filled with God's promises, with over 300 'promise' verses you can turn to in your time of need. God's promises assure us how much He cares about us in our circumstance. He wants us to know that He is committed. God's promises show who God is: Protector. Counselor. Provider. Restorer. Comforter. Deliverer.

Promises are seen when health is restored (Jeremiah 30:17), when prayers are answered (Isaiah 65:24), and when feeling unloved (Romans 8:38-39) or discouraged (Joshua 1:9). When we embrace the promises of God, we get to see and know God. Knowing God brings you to the most essential point of living and being: to worship God.

Worship exemplifies valued worthiness. Worship makes God the happiest. It is more than getting dressed up and going to church service once a week or, for those on the Christmas and Easter schedule, twice a year. Worship is what you do every day, every minute, every second in your words, deeds, thoughts, behavior, and even in your habits. It is a song. It is a prayer with and for another person. It is meditating on God's Word. It is acknowledging living by the grace of God. And it is you being the fruit of the Spirit (Galatians 5:22-23). In your worship, you are making a promise to God to connect your spirit to His.

God is worthy to be praised and His promises to embrace!

Charlotte Diakite

Record your Notes or Reflections:
What is God's promise that you need today?
How will you express your promise to worship?

_____

_____

_____

_____

_____

_____

_____

_____

_____

You Are in The Lord's Plan

"Where can I go from your Spirit? Where can I flee from your presence?"
- Psalm 139:7, New International Version

Jehovah has a plan for each of us, a plan that is traced from the day we were born until the day He calls us to His presence. Throughout our lifetime, we go through both good times and rough times, and we have to learn from them.

Sometimes, we don't believe in ourselves. We think that we are not capable of facing our daily challenges, so we try to escape. We have to believe that each situation the Lord put us in is His way to refine us to make us stronger to confront any difficulty. Do not worry, because we are facing that road filled with adverse circumstances while holding His hand.

We are not alone. Jehovah walks with us every step of the way, leading us to be better people and better Christians. Look around you. There is no storm that comes in front of us that we cannot overcome, because our Father is in control and will help us come out victorious. Let our Lord take control of every moment in our lives, and the results will amaze us.

Trust in the Lord. He will never let us down, nor forsake us. Our Father is the answer for all of our questions, for all of our anguish, so sit down and talk to Him, and tell Him what you want. What you need will be granted according to His will. "Ask and I will give it to you," said the Lord, so don't be afraid, find the way, the time, and the place where you are going to connect with God.

Mirian Cukovic

Record your Notes or Reflections:

When was the last time you sat to talk to God?

How did He answer you?

_____

_____

_____

_____

_____

_____

_____

_____

_____

_____

_____

Depending on God

"I am the vine, you are the branches. If you remain in me and I in you, you will bear much fruit; apart from me you can do nothing." - John 15:5, New International Version

When we depend on God, we are trusting Him to fulfill His promises to us. Dependence is a continual connection to Christ that results in a harvest of holiness. What do you think God is saying when He says you will bear much fruit? The fruits of the spirit are love, peace, joy, kindness, goodness, faithfulness, gentleness, and self-control. This is the kind of fruit that never goes bad. It's always fresh and perfectly ripened.

Many times, you will hear people say life does not come with an instruction manual, but that's not true! It does, and it's called *The Holy Bible*. Anything and everything that we've been through and what is still yet to come, is in that book. When we pray, we depend on God to answer our prayers. Prayer is the direct line of communication between us and Jesus, who intercedes on our behalf. Our faith is increased, our strength is renewed, and peace becomes still. When we depend on God, we see His power working in our lives. Plant seeds of faith, then water them with the word of God. Store the good fruits of the spirit in your bowl that God gives to those who depend on Him. Let your harvest become bountiful as you trust God to supply all your needs.

Veniss Aguilerra

Record your Notes or Reflections:

During this season, how often are you communicating with God? In what areas of your life are you depending on God to provide your needs?

_____

_____

_____

_____

_____

_____

_____

_____

_____

_____

_____

_____

_____

Obedience Always Brings Blessings

"Does the Lord delight in burnt offerings and sacrifices as much as in obeying the Lord? To obey is better than sacrifice..." - 1 Samuel 15:22, New International Version

When our lives are going well, being obedient is easy. However, when we have difficulties, such as problems with our health or family, work, or other needs, it is really difficult to obey.

Obedience has to be the first priority in the life of a Christian. It is the only way that we can achieve all the extraordinary things God has prepared for us. The Holy Spirit will help us walk obediently before God. We must choose to obey Him, even if we cannot understand what God asks us to do. We have to have faith in His direction, which is always the best for us. Jeremiah 29:11 says, "For I know the plans I have for you, declares the Lord, plans to prosper you and not to harm you, plans to give you hope and a future."

In God's plan for our lives, being obedient is vital. God will use His Word, as well as messages from pastors, other people, or He will speak to us through the Holy Spirit to continue in the guidance of obedience. God knows that obeying Him is a challenge, but we must follow the example of Jesus, who was obedient until death.

When we obey God, He blesses us. Why? Because obedience always brings blessings. So, let's set a goal of obeying God and watching Him work in our lives.

Ingrid Quevedo

Record your Notes or Reflections:

In what area in your life is God telling you to be obedient?

_____

_____

_____

_____

_____

_____

_____

_____

_____

_____

_____

_____

_____

_____

_____

_____

Comforted by the Father of Compassion

"Praise be to the God and Father of our Lord Jesus Christ, the Father of compassion and the God of all comfort, who comforts us in all our troubles, so that we can comfort those in any trouble with the comfort we ourselves received from God." - 2 Corinthians 1:3-4, New International Version

On Wednesday, January 8, 2020, at 6:45 PM, a day before my birthday, my loving father was called home to be with the Lord. My mom asked me to stay home with her and not attend the church meeting scheduled that night. She did not want me to leave her side, so I stayed home. There was no coincidence in that decision. I believe God willed for me to be home that evening. He gave me the opportunity to speak to my dad, pray with him, tell him I loved him, kiss him, tell him that it was okay to rest, that Jesus Himself held him in His arms. I positioned my dad to face my mom. He looked at her and she knew that his end was near, as she began to exclaim, "He's leaving, he's leaving!"

Sure enough, moments later, my dad took his last breath. He looked so peaceful. I remember lifting my hands towards heaven and thanking God. I thanked Him for allowing me to be present and tell my dad for the last time that I loved him. I prayed for God's peace that surpasses all understanding and for comfort for my family and for myself. During the wake and entombment, I had such peace in my heart. I knew my heavenly Father was sustaining me and comforting me. Father's Day, my dad's birthday, and now the holidays that are coming, I know that I will be comforted by the God of all comfort.

Thank you, Jesus, for continuing to comfort me during this time of loss. Help me to comfort and express compassion for others that have experienced loss in their life. Amen.

Maria Rivera

Record your Notes or Reflections:
Loss is never easy. Have you had a loss in your life?
Who has given you comfort?

_____

_____

_____

_____

_____

_____

_____

_____

The 5th Season; The Season of Job

"In the land of Uz, there lived a man whose name was Job. This man was blameless and upright; he feared God and shunned evil." - Job: 1:1, New International Version

"The Lord blessed the latter part of Job's life more than the former part." - Job: 42: 12, New International Version

During fall, the leaves are bursting with the colors of the season - brilliant oranges, reds, and yellows. Depending on your location, there might even be more leaves on the ground than there are on the branches. What might the seasons of our lives resemble?

Winter is a time when things are dormant. Though we may not see very much growth on the outside, God is moving, and seeds are growing beneath the surface. Spring always conjures up new life and the bursting forth of dreams, plans, and purposes. Summer is a time of harvest and flourishing, and Fall is "the last hurrah" before rest comes.

But I started to think of another season in our lives - the Job season. This season is unpredictable and comes out of nowhere and often by no fault of our own. This is a season that can literally bring you to your knees.

Job was a man described as blameless and righteous, but despite his spirit and character, he endured horrific calamity. We know that it rains on the just and the unjust alike, and God is no respecter of persons. I can't imagine the kind of faith and reverence it took to refuse to curse God in the midst of Job's suffering. I can't imagine having my tribe and my spouse speaking words of discouragement and despair while I suffer, but there are times we are called to stand our ground alone.

Could you? Could you continue to praise and worship The Father during relentless attacks and horrific calamity in your life? Could you stand your ground? It takes a supernatural faith to trust and honor God like Job. God knew His child and He knows you too. If The Father allows it, He'll equip you to get through the other side to your victory. Stand your ground, Beloved, and watch God bless your latter days too!

Joyce Travers-Johnson

Record your Notes or Reflections:

Has there been a season in your life when everything seemed to fall apart all at once?

Think of a time when your call for help fell upon deaf ears and how you responded. Did you curse God and ask Him why, or did you press in and stand your ground?

Like Job, we really can do ALL things through the strength of The Father.

_____

_____

_____

Heart of Giving

"Each of you should give what you have decided in your heart to give, not reluctantly or under compulsion, for God loves a cheerful giver. And God is able to bless you abundantly, so that in all things at all times, having all that you need, you will abound in every good work." - 2 Corinthians 9:7-8, New International Version

Know that when you give, God richly rewards. Did you know that He doesn't need money? What He wants is for you to give your best, your last, your everything with a heart of thanksgiving. Giving is not just a monetary action, but also a physical and emotional state. God has blessed you with gifts, each uniquely given to you before you were born. As you develop the gifts in you, they are to be shared with others, that all may see the glory of God in you. As you give of your time, He will reward you with time. As you give financially, He will take care of your financial needs. It doesn't matter the size or amount of the giving; what matters is what's in your heart. A heart full of love and praise is worth more than silver and gold.

Therefore, do not worry about your worldly goods, as they will have no purpose in life eternal, where you will be rich and have the best of everything. While on earth, you are to give to those less fortunate than you - a meal, shelter, clothing, and hope. To those who do not know God and have lost hope, give them prayer, an invitation to a church, bible study, and a bible. You give what has been given to you and the light within you will shine from within you for all to see. No matter your circumstance, no matter how you are feeling when you give from your heart, you give God the glory.

Keila Vera

Record your Notes or Reflections:

Are there areas in your life where you need to give?

Where and why?

How has your way(s) of giving impacted your life?

_____

_____

_____

_____

_____

_____

_____

_____

_____

_____

You Are not Alone

"…Because God has said, never will I leave you; never will I forsake you."
- Hebrews 13:5b, New International Version

Nowadays, in our society, loneliness is a real problem. Even with all the social media available at our fingertips, people still feel alone. However, as Christians, even though we may sometimes be physically alone, we are not, because we know that God is with us.

My wife, Ingrid, would spend many hours alone at home while I spent long hours at work in the hospital. Her family would wonder how she was able to be alone for so long, but she would tell them that God was with her, keeping her company.

Jesus said that He would not leave us alone when He said in Matthew 28:20, "And surely I am with you always, to the very end of the age." Do we need to be concerned that we can be separated from God? Absolutely not! I am reassured by the following verse in Romans 8:38-39 - "I am persuaded, that neither death, nor life, nor angels, nor principalities, nor powers, nor things present, nor things to come, nor height, nor depth, nor any other creature, shall be able to separate us from the love of God, which is in Christ Jesus our Lord."

We are not alone, and we cannot be separated from God or His love. As long as we are with God, Jesus, we are never alone, no matter what the world is going through, with its feelings of isolation, loneliness, and emptiness. We are with God and nothing in this world can separate us from the love of God. Therefore, we are comforted in knowing that we are never alone when we believe in Jesus, because He loves us and is with us.

Jonathan Quevedo

Record your Notes or Reflections:
Do you ever feel alone?
How does knowing that God will never leave you give you reassurance?

_____

_____

_____

_____

_____

_____

_____

_____

_____

Ask God for What You Need

"If you then, being evil, know how to give good gifts to your children, how much more will your Father who is in heaven give good things to those who ask Him!" - Matthew 7:11 (New King James Version)

Parents want to make their children happy, but parents do not always give their children what they ask for, either because they cannot, or because it does not suit the child. But if children ask for what is right and good, they will most likely receive it. We must have this same trust in God, because He is good and generous.

When we limit ourselves and trust only our abilities, we fail, but when we focus on our faith in what God can do, we discover an infinite supply of joy.

God's very nature assures us of His provision. He is omniscient, omnipotent, and omnipresent.

Sometimes, we try to meet our own needs without asking God, but that never works. It only leads to frustration and deep disappointment.

Why do we want to obtain things for ourselves and not ask God for them? James 4:2 says, "But you do not have what you want, because you do not ask." If we ask God for something, He will give it to us if it is according to His will. Many times, we have to wait, because God knows what the best time is to receive it.

When we have needs, let us ask God, because if it is correct, He will give it to us at the right time. If it is not correct, He will give us something much better than what we asked for. If our parents try to give us what we desire, how much more would our Heavenly Father, who is perfect, also give to us?

God solved our biggest problem when Jesus came to earth and died for us. Don't we think He cares about the other problems we are going through? Absolutely!

He cares about our health, family, finances, and more. God cares about the needs of His children, and that includes you and me.

Ingrid Quevedo

Record your Notes or Reflections:
What do you need that you have not asked God for?

_____

_____

_____

_____

_____

_____

_____

_____

There is Power in Your Praise

"Now when they began to sing and to praise, the LORD set ambushes against the people of Ammon, Moab, and Mount Seir, who had come against Judah; and they were defeated." - 2 Chronicles 20:22, New King James Version

Three nations, with a great multitude in their army, conspired to come against the nation of Judah. Given advanced warning, King Jehoshaphat faced the message of this attack against Judah with a natural response of fear, but his supernatural response to fast and SEEK GOD kicked in. This response ushered in God's miraculous defeat of the enemy, making them set ambush amongst themselves. Think about that - the Lord not only saved Judah by making the enemy take their focus off of God's people, He also caused them to defeat and kill others who were coming up against them, too.

I personally witnessed this miracle in my life. Unbeknownst to me, a few people were conspiring against me from being nominated and selected as the President on a Board. At the moment of decision, the person chosen to come against me is the one whom God used to grant me favor to become President. This confused the individuals that the person conspired with. I had no knowledge of this, yet my spirit was already in action concerning the situation, praying for God's Will and praising Him.

Later, when I was told about the conspiracy, I smiled, knowing God's hand was completely in control of the situation, covering me. I witnessed Romans 8:31 in full effect, "...If God is for us, who can be against us?" God will use the enemy coming against you to defeat others who come up against you. Think about the power of that promise.

I encourage you to read King Jehoshaphat's account in 2 Chronicles 20:1-30. You will discover the simple strategy he used in his darkest hour: SEEK GOD, speak GOD's Word, hear and believe the promise of GOD's victory, and PRAISE GOD!

There were no drills at the army camp, inventory and collection of weapons, or situation room conferences in King Jehoshaphat's story. The Lord set ambush against the enemies of Judah and the operative words prior to that are, "When they began to sing and to praise." What a powerful strategy we can use to this day knowing there is power in our praise.

Candi Young

Record your Notes or Reflections:
What's hindering you from putting King Jehoshaphat's strategy into action?
When have you praised God during a storm?
What was the outcome?

_____

_____

_____

Confidence in Christ

"So we may boldly say: The Lord is my helper, I will not fear. What can man do to me?" - Hebrews 13:6, English Standard Version

Confidence in Christ produces spiritual boldness. I thank God for the trials I have been through that brought me to where I am today because through each trial and tribulation, He kept me. He didn't have to choose me, but He did, and I choose Him in return. I walk out of my house daily fully armored. I say yes to the call of God. I say, "Here I am Lord, send me." Not for my own honor, but because of my confidence in Christ.

I encourage you to put all your faith and all your confidence in Christ Jesus. He is the only one who laid down his sinless life so that you may live with the one who created you. Build up your spiritual confidence so that you can go boldly to the throne of grace and get up knowing that God is working on your behalf, for your greater good.

Nothing can separate us from the love of God, so what is there to fear? Fear is not of God; He tells us over and over to be courageous. We are created in His image. Of all the things Jesus faced, He never once said, "Father, I'm scared." He was on a mission from God and did what He had to do, no matter what the situation was. His confidence was in His Father. Let us be Christ-like and not let anything distract us from fulfilling the will of God.

Veniss Aguilerra

Record your Notes or Reflections:

How are you building up your confidence in Christ during this season?

In what areas of your life are you letting fear hold you back?

_____

_____

_____

_____

_____

_____

_____

_____

_____

_____

_____

_____

_____

Obedience

"Teach me to do your will, for you are my God; may your good Spirit lead me on level ground." - Psalm 143:10, New International Version

What is doing God's will? What does God want us to do? God has told us to be righteous, to forgive, and to love. Being righteous is about walking through life doing the right thing. The dictionary defines the righteous as one who works according to justice. According to the circumstances presented to us in life, we must make decisions that even if they go against ourselves, we have to do what our conscience dictates to us, knowing that our conscience is the voice of God who tells us to do the right thing.

God has told us to forgive, to have a generous heart, to extend our hands to those who need it, but especially to those who might not coincide with us in any way in our daily lives, or simply do not think like us.

Jehovah wants us to be examples of life just as Jesus was when He was on earth.

God is love, and Jesus was in our midst to teach us to love our neighbor. God wants us to love each other just as He loves us. Love is the basis for any relationship; from parents to children, between friends, between couples. Love is worrying about each other's well-being, and that is what Jesus teaches us. Let Jehovah take us by the hand and guide us on what He wants us to do, which is His will. Glory to God.

Mirian Cukovic

Record your Notes or Reflections:
Reflect and write about a situation in your life that made you be obedient or disobedient to God's will for your life.

_____

_____

_____

_____

_____

_____

_____

_____

_____

_____

_____

Created to Fit

"Each board had two tenons for binding one to another." - Exodus 36:22,
New King James Version

The tenons, or boards, that built the tabernacle in the Old
Testament were equally measured and cut to fit into each other.
Similarly, this is also how God has designed your life. People will
come and go at various stages of growth from birth through
adulthood. You will meet so many people along your path, but
not all are meant to FIT. Throughout your life, you will create
bonds, relationships, friendships at school, work, church, with
people from all walks of life. When those bonds that you created
and cherished have dissolved, you are left with hurt, pain, and
anguish.

God has a hand in everything pertaining to your life—who will
come, who will stay, and who will go. The reasons why those
people are no longer a part of your life is because God's plan is
greater than what you can imagine, and those people are not part
of the blueprint. People come into your life to help you along the
path. They each deposit something that will spark what is already
inside of you to allow you to discover your purpose. Everyone
won't FIT because your piece is uniquely made by God. He
carefully selected all the materials to create you and therefore, only
other unique pieces will be compatible to FIT. The removal of the
pieces isn't to hurt you, it doesn't mean that there is anything

wrong with you; it's simply making way for the right FIT. You need to trust God.

Let Go and Let God.

Keila Vera

Record your Notes or Reflections:
What areas of your life do you need to trust God?

_____

_____

_____

_____

_____

_____

_____

_____

_____

_____

I AM a New Creation

"Therefore, if anyone is in Christ, he is a new creation; old things have passed away; behold, all things have become new." - 2 Corinthians 5:17 New King James Version

As I walked towards the "plus size" section of the store, I couldn't help but notice the mannequins adorned in the rich colors of the new season. For a moment, I thought maybe I could find something in the regular section, but that thought was short-lived as my mind space reverted back to the usual mantra - *It's okay if you can't find anything.* Suddenly, the mission was halted as I caught a glance at myself in the mirror. You see, I'm not one to try on clothing and then marvel at the end product. It's quite the contrary, as I've been betrayed by the scale for most of my adult life. But this time was different. I slowly took a few steps backwards and stared at a stranger staring back at me. I didn't recognize her, and she didn't appear to recognize me. I knew I lost weight and purchased clothing two sizes smaller, but this was so unfamiliar, it was uncomfortable. My outward appearance had been transformed, but I still viewed myself through the eyes of a woman who was several sizes larger. Little did I know, the inward battle wasn't going to be as easy as making the physical changes, and I would be called to extend grace to myself through the process.

Sometimes, I think we're like that with God. Even after we've accepted Christ as our Lord and savior, we continue to view ourselves from the rearview mirror. If the changes in our heart don't immediately come together with the outward appearance, we're ready to throw in the towel. At the first misstep, the crowd is in line, poised to judge through the lens of condemnation, examining our every move. What kind of Christian are you, they ask?

Well, Beloved, you're the kind of Christian who is imperfectly perfect. You're the kind of Christian who said yes and is allowing the Father to lovingly walk you through the process of getting to know Him. Just like I decided to become healthier, you decided to accept Him, and then the work began. As you draw closer to Him, your heart, character, and vision become more and more like God's. You've got to see yourself through the eyes of the Father and meditate on who HE says you are now. The old man has died. You are a new creation!

Joyce Travers-Johnson

Record your Notes or Reflections:
Over the past year, how have you changed on the outside?
Now, how has God changed you on the inside?
Are you seeing yourself from a "God's eye" view?

_____

_____

_____

_____

Choose Life

"For you created my inmost being; you knit me together in my mother's womb." - Psalm 139:13, New International Version

We live in a society where very little value is given to human life, especially when it comes to unplanned pregnancies outside of the sanctity of marriage. Abortion is viewed as a solution to an unwanted pregnancy. A choice is made to terminate human life.

The Bible warns of sexual immorality, found in 1 Corinthians 7:2 and Galatians 5:19. The consequences of sexual immorality are suffered largely by the unborn babies that are being killed in the womb. If you find yourself having to make a decision to terminate the life in your womb, may you prayerfully and earnestly consider other alternatives. If you are unable to keep the child, pray that God would bring you a childless couple that desires to have, love, and raise a child.

Today, I am a grandmother because the choice of life was made. Against uncertainty, against opposition, and against a far too common practice, my daughter chose life. My grandchildren are a promise, with many possibilities and potentialities for the Kingdom of God. They are heirs to His Kingdom! As are all children! "Let the little children come to me, and do not hinder them, for the Kingdom of God belongs to such as these." (Luke 18:16, New International Version)

If you find yourself in a situation where you have to make a tough decision regarding the life in your womb, may I encourage you to call on God and make this your prayer: Jesus, give me the wisdom and courage to make the right choice and birth what you created and knit together in my womb. Amen.

Maria Rivera

Record your Notes or Reflections:
What difficult decisions do you have to bring before God?

_____

_____

_____

_____

_____

_____

_____

_____

_____

_____

Jesus is a Gentleman

"Here I am! I stand at the door and knock. If anyone hears my voice and opens the door, I will come in and eat with that person, and they with me." - Revelation 3:20, New International Version

The Merriam-Webster Dictionary defines a gentleman as:

- a man of noble birth;

- a man who combines noble birth or rank with chivalrous qualities; or

- a man whose conduct conforms to a high standard of propriety or correct behavior.

Jesus, who is the all-powerful Creator of the Universe, and who can do anything that He wants to, is the best symbol of a "gentleman." He is of noble birth - the King of Kings. The all-powerful who stands at the door and knocks, waiting for us to open it for Him. Although He could easily break down the door or go through it, He does not force Himself on us.

Jesus can easily go through locked doors. Multiple times, the Bible cites that the disciples were hiding with the doors locked for fear of the Jewish leaders. And in both instances, Jesus came and stood among them. Jesus did not force Himself onto his disciples. He already had a relationship with them. Jesus came in, in spite of the locked doors, because He knew He would be welcomed.

Our almighty and all-powerful Jesus, the King of Kings, is a gentleman in the purest sense of the word. May we all be of the same character to follow the example of our Lord and Savior, strive to show correct behavior at all times, and be thankful for his shining light.

Jonathan Quevedo

Record your Notes or Reflections:

How does it make you feel that God will never force His will upon you?

_____

_____

_____

_____

_____

_____

_____

_____

_____

_____

The Importance of Forgiveness

"For if you forgive other people when they sin against you, your heavenly Father will also forgive you. But if you do not forgive others their sins, your Father will not forgive your sins." - Matthew 6:14-15, New International Version

"Give us today our daily bread," (Matthew 6:11) means give us today what we need. By giving us our daily bread, it also means we must think about all the things that we have, and be very grateful to God, because He is the one who has given us everything we need. Remember, there are things that we can live without. We do not need electronics, cars, or toys to survive. Those are considered the things we want. The things we need can be considered those things needed for survival. Forgiveness is key to our spiritual survival.

"And forgive us our debts, as we also forgive our debtors." (Matthew 6:12) We are encouraged to apologize for our mistakes. To ask for forgiveness means that we are sorry for something we did, and that we will not do it again. At the same time, we also have to forgive others who may have done us wrong. Sometimes, they offend us intentionally, while other times, unintentionally. But we must pray to God and ask for help in order to forgive others. When we forgive others, God forgives us.

Prayer is a special way to talk to God. Remember to pray as many times as necessary. God wants us, you, and me, and He wants to hear from us daily. He already knows our struggles, our needs, and our wants because He is God. All He wants you, us, me is to get to know Him intimately.

Vilma Tricoche

Record your Notes or Reflections:

Who do you need to forgive today?

What do you need forgiveness for; from God, another person, or yourself?

_____

_____

_____

_____

_____

_____

_____

_____

_____

_____

_____

Gratitude Attitude

"Give thanks to the Lord, for He is good, for His steadfast love endures forever." - New International Version, Psalm 107:1

There are two words children are taught when a parent asks them, "What do you say?" For parents, it is so pleasing to hear the response - "Thank you."

As a child of God, the Heavenly Father is pleased with thank you. However, your thanks transcend beyond two words. Your thank you is your worship of God. It is a lifestyle defined by your thoughts, behaviors, actions, and the words you say or share. In other words, the extent of expressing thanks reflects your Gratitude Attitude. Through a Gratitude Attitude, your thank you makes you ready and willing to show appreciation, empowers you to sow bridges, tear down walls, and create an environment where peace and fellowship may flourish. You exude a gratefulness in feeling blessed because God gives you another chance.

Cultivate a gratitude attitude

Pray. Bring everything you've got to God.

Count Your Blessings. List each of God's goodness.

Say Thank You. Send a thank-you card, email, texts, or share your smile.

Gratitude Attitude Challenge

Every day for the next seven days:

Morning - **Pray**. Pray God's Word (Scripture) and write out your scripture verse(s) for that day.

Mid-Day - **Count Your Blessings**. Take one minute and list examples of God's goodness.

End of the Day - **Say Thank You** to someone (different someone each day) through a card, email, text, or a smile. *Extra Bonus:* Express your thanks to someone(s) you really do not want to thank.

Charlotte Diakite

Gratitude Attitude Challenge. Ready? Set? Go. WHAT DO YOU SAY? Write out the information below for seven days.

Day_____
Scripture Prayer:
Blessings Count:
Say Thank You:

Dear ( ),

On the seventh day, the Lord says well done!

_____

_____

_____

I Am Not Troubled

"But when you hear of wars and rumors of wars, do not be troubled; for such things must happen, but the end is not yet." Mark 13:7, New King James Version

God expects us to be at peace in the midst of the storm. He warns us not to be overwhelmed with fear of war, or the showing of the signs of the last days. These things MUST take place. We are commissioned to continue to spread the gospel even in the midst of turmoil, not get caught up in it. The only way to do this is to focus on God.

My late mother would say to me, if she wasn't around and "these things" began to happen, that I should only fret if my relationship with God was in question. She would then tell me to only fret a moment and get into action to SEEK GOD. A month before my dad passed away, he adamantly told me to get my life right with God because He was the only way. This, I would expect more from my mother than my father.

Reflecting years later, I appreciate my earthly parents reinforcing a parental directive from our Heavenly Father. The year 2020 hit us with a pandemic that made me reflect on Mark 13:7 and my parents' words. It was time to BE STILL (Psalms 46:10). As I became physically, mentally, and spiritually still, I reflected on my relationship with the Lord. I didn't assess it by my church attendance, nor by my ability to recite scriptures and teach the Word, nor my ministerial service in the Kingdom. I assessed it by how close of a relationship I had with God and whether I was a human "BEing" or human "DOing". Where was my peace? (Philippians 4:6-7) Was I abiding in the Lord? (John 15:1-8)

It was a lamenting heart check; an assessment of my relationship with God and my obedience to His Will for my life. In this reflection, 2020 gave me a clear vision of my life in spite of the troubling things happening. I had to excuse myself from quite a few initiatives to BE STILL as I took my parents' life-saving directive to SEEK GOD. In this, I found peace, a message of hope, and direction. I AM NOT TROUBLED because I abide in Christ and He abides in me!

Candi Young

Record your Notes or Reflections:
What is troubling you that you need to SEEK GOD and take to prayer?

_____

_____

_____

_____

_____

_____

Obedience

"But Samuel replied, What is more pleasing to the Lord: your burnt offerings and sacrifices or your obedience to his voice? Listen! Obedience is better than sacrifice, and submission is better than offering the fat of rams." - 1 Samuel 15:22, New Living Translation

Why is obedience to God important? From Genesis to Revelation, the Bible has a lot to say about obedience. In the story of the Ten Commandments, we see how important the concept is to God.

In the New Testament, we learn through the example of Jesus Christ that believers are called to a life of compliance. The Bible defines this as listening to a higher authority. The following five reasons will help us to understand:

1. **Jesus calls us to listen to the Lord.** In Jesus Christ, we find the perfect model. As his disciples, we follow the example of Christ and His Commandments. Our motivation is love. "If you love me, keep my commands." (John 14:15, New International Version)

2. **Obedience is an act of worship.** The Bible says that believers are not justified by obedience. Salvation is a gift from God, and we can do nothing to deserve it. True Christian compliance flows through the grace we have received from the Lord. "Therefore, I urge you, brothers and sisters, in view of God's mercy, to offer your bodies as a living sacrifice, holy and pleasing to God- this is your true and proper worship." (Romans 12:1, New International Version)

3. **God rewards our servitude to Him.** The Bible says, "...all nations on earth will be blessed, because you have obeyed me." (Genesis 22:18, New International Version)

4. **Serving God tests our love.** Loving God implies following His commandments. God has commanded us to love one another, such as in John 15:12.

5. **Obedience to God shows faith.** When we obey God, we show our trust and faith in Him. When we disobey God, we are in rebellion. That has consequences, just as what happened to King Saul. "For rebellion *is as* the sin of witchcraft, and stubbornness *is as* iniquity and idolatry. Because you have rejected the word of the LORD, He also has rejected you from *being* king." (1 Samuel 15:23, New King James Version)

There are many more defining moments of obedience in the Bible. Wisdom tells us to pay attention and listen to God. Lord, help us to be obedient to Your purpose and plan for our lives. Amen.

Vilma Tricoche

Record your Notes or Reflections:
In what ways can you be obedient to God?

_____

_____

_____

_____

Waiting on God and His Perfect Timing

"...If it seems slow, do not despair, for these things will surely come to pass. Just be patient! They will not be overdue a single day!" - Habakkuk 2: 3, The Living Bible

We are living in a world of speed, and when we have to wait in any circumstance, it causes impatience, frustrations, and we make wrong decisions. We want the good things in our lives, and we want to have them immediately.

We know that God uses those moments of waiting to teach us great lessons that will be blessings and give Him glory.

God has His own sense of time, because to the Lord, one day is a thousand years, and a thousand years is one day. (2 Peter 3:8)

God has perfect timing; He is never early, nor never late. He is never rushed. However, God is always punctual.

God loves each one of us, and promises to answer all our requests, but does not give it to us in our time. He knows the perfect time from start to finish. In the time we are waiting, God will produce qualities and characters that will help us carry out His will. Sometimes, we want to manipulate our circumstances. The problem is that when we make our own arrangements, we are placed outside of God's will, and we eventually have to live with the negative consequences.

Sometimes, we want to pressure God to do something for us when He tells us "no." God is protecting us. He is not rejecting. He only wants the best for us. God is good and loves us unconditionally. He wants to give to us more bountifully and do things much more abundantly than we ask for or understand. (Ephesians 3:20)

Our waiting is always rewarded, not in the time that we want or think we need. Let's give God time to change and do His work, and allow Him the time to make everything work for the good of us.

Ingrid Quevedo

Record your Notes or Reflections:
In what ways do you find it hard to wait for God's response?

_____

_____

_____

_____

_____

_____

_____

_____

Get Started Again

"Rise up; this matter is in your hands. We will support you, so take courage and do it." - Ezra 10:4, New International Version

Ezra was challenged to return to Jerusalem after his exile to Babylon and rebuild it, not only spiritually, but to rebuild the city that was in ruins. The task was not easy.

The first thing was to remove the debris, then start building the houses. How many times have we found ourselves in situations where we have been morally finished, without money and with debts that are almost impossible to pay? You have fallen into depression, anxiety, gotten sick, and you've noticed that you hit rock bottom, that you can't go any further down.

When we are at the bottom of the cliff, all we have left is to look up and start climbing. But how do you do it if you don't have any resources to support your climb? All you need is to have faith, because our Father is there to take over.

There is a phrase that says "Faith moves mountains." For God, the impossible becomes possible. As human beings, we fear the ability to recognize that our Father is at the forefront of everything. If you don't have, it's because you don't ask. Raise your eyes to the Father and you can witness God's miracles in your life. A new beginning is right in front of you. Be courageous and take the first step to a life full of peace with security that each step will be one step closer to the glory of God.

How beautiful is it to have the conviction to know that we are not alone, that we are always in the shadow of a God who shelters us, that there will be no storm we cannot overcome with the help of our Father. Remember, faith doesn't make things easy - it makes them possible.

Don't hesitate to seek the Lord in times of disgrace. He is always ready to start a new beginning with you. The Lord's grace is amazing. Just close your eyes, raise your hands, connect with Him, be quiet, be silent, and listen. He is talking to you.

Don't forget that Jesus is walking with you in good times and bad. He is always there with His hands protecting you.

Mirian Cukovic

Record your Notes or Reflections:
Reflect and write about a discouraging situation where you needed to start again. Do you need to start again now? What steps you need to take?

_____

_____

_____

_____

_____

Prayer of Salvation

ROMANS ROADS TO SALVATION

Romans Road to Salvation explains the good news of salvation using verses from the Book of Romans. It is a powerful method of explaining why we need salvation, how God provided salvation, how we can receive salvation, and the results of salvation.

Romans 3:10, 3:23, 5:12 – All have sinned

Romans 6:23 – The consequences of sin

Romans 5:8 – God's demonstrated love for us

Romans 10:9-13 – Confess Jesus Christ as our Lord and Savior

Romans 5:1, 8:1, 8:38-39 – No condemnation, peace with and connected to God

PRAYER OF SALVATION

Your journey starts with a prayer and belief in Jesus! Remember, no one can come to the Father except through the Son; "Jesus said to him, "I am the way, the truth, and the life. No one comes to the Father except through Me." John 14:6 New King James Version. The Seeking God Club invites you to pray the prayer of salvation below. This prayer is a first step to come in agreement with God about your sin and accept His gift of salvation.

Father God, I repent and come before you asking for forgiveness of my sins. I BELIEVE Jesus died for my sins and rose from the dead. I confess Jesus Christ as my Lord and Savior and today, I invite Him and the Holy Spirit to come into my heart and into my life to help me. Thank You for accepting me and giving me the gift of eternal life. In Jesus name I pray, Amen

If you prayed that for the first time, CONGRATULATIONS, Heaven is rejoicing and so is SGC. We invite you to send an email to sgcpray@gmail.com. The prayer team would like to pray for you and offer any support you may need to guide you on your journey. God bless you!

The Seeking God Club

Record your Notes or Reflections:
Write your personal prayer of repentance and surrender, accepting Jesus as your Savior.

_____

_____

_____

_____

_____

_____

_____

Meet the Writers

CANDI YOUNG is the visionary leader of the Seeking God Club (SGC) and this guided journal. Her Kingdom assignment is to develop leaders personally, professionally, and mentor them in ministerial servitude to the Lord. Candi has a perpetual hunger to receive and teach God's Word; it is through SGC leadership that God is satisfying her heart's desire. As a Chaplain and Life Purpose Coach, her mission is to connect people to God and their God-given purpose. This assignment brings others to personal awareness, inspired growth, and transformation towards living a fulfilled life. This has been a Spirit-led passion for Candi, having overcome a dark season of depression, anxiety, and suicidal thoughts in 2011. Not understanding her purpose and her God perpetuated the crisis during that season.

Candi loves to worship and commune with the Lord for strength. She adores time with her two adult sons, Brandon and Timothy, as well as with family and friends. One of her favorite scriptures is Romans 8:28, "And we know that all things work together for good to those who love God, to those who are the called according to His purpose."

CHARLOTTE M. DIAKITE is a co-founding leader of SGC. Her heart's passion is ministry that meets women "at the crossroad."

She is a teacher, facilitator, mentor, consultant, and speaker who serves in several ministries and advocacy groups. As a female small business owner, Charlotte unapologetically puts "God first" in her work and leadership. She loves her church family fellowship. Moreover, Charlotte loves sharing the gospel and being the church.

Diagnosed with lupus in 2017, Charlotte saw her life story re-scripted. Going through immense physical and emotional pain in the early days of this chronic illness journey, she found herself at the crossroad: searching, questioning and even contemplating. Seeking God became even more important.

Hailing from Brooklyn, New York, Charlotte now resides in New Jersey. She cherishes her family and lifetime friends. Charlotte enjoys gardening with her husband, Ab, watching Marvel movies with her son, Yussef, and creating music with her daughter, Fatima.

With her life story having been many times 're-scripted,' while at the crossroad, one of Charlotte's favorite faith scripture is Jeremiah 29:11, "'I know the plans I have for you,' declares the Lord, 'plans to prosper you and not to harm you, plans to give you hope and a future.'"

INGRID QUEVEDO is a dentist from the Dominican Republic. Ingrid joined as a leader in the Seeking God Club with the main focus on touching the hearts of those who speak Spanish. Knowing the desire of her heart, God opened the door for Ingrid to pioneer a Spanish-speaking Bible Study group with her local church. She also leads a Spanish-speaking subset of the women's ministry at her church.

Ingrid and her husband Jonathan have a burning desire to go and help those in need. Ingrid uses her dental skills with going on medical mission trips to South American countries to provide care and the message of Jesus for those who are in need. Ingrid also enjoys spending the early morning hours in prayer and communication with God. Ingrid's favorite scripture verse is Joshua 1:9, New International Version, "Have I not commanded you? Be strong and courageous. Do not be afraid; do not be discouraged, for the LORD your God will be with you wherever you go."

JONATHAN QUEVEDO is a retired physician with a specialty in Physical Medicine and Rehabilitation. He retired after his wife Ingrid told him that, after praying, she heard from God that he should. Jonathan obeyed God and now has the time to do His work. Jonathan became a Seeking God Club leader, teaching via the conference call line as well as teaching videos on SGC's online platform. Jonathan, who speaks Spanish, is also involved with his wife leading a weekly Spanish-speaking Bible Study group through their local Church. Using his medical background, he also shows how evolution does not make sense and that Biblical creation is the origin of life.

Jonathan and his wife have a desire, and go on medical mission trips to South American countries to talk directly to the people, address their medical and dental needs, and spread the message of the love of God. Jonathan's favorite scripture verse is Philippians 4:8, New International Version, "Finally, brothers and sister, whatever is true, whatever is noble, whatever is right, whatever is pure, whatever is lovely, whatever is admirable- if anything is excellent or praiseworthy - think about such things."

JOYCE TRAVERS-JOHNSON is a dynamic worship leader and Chaplain who understands the power of worship in releasing healing and deliverance to those who need a "touch from the Lord." As a Seeking God Club Leader, she often ministers through the "I AM" series, declaring who we are in Christ. In 2019, out of her fervent desire to help the homeless and hungry, the "GO Project Ministry" was launched. She, along with a group of volunteers, take to the streets and offer meals and ministry to the hurting, homeless, and hungry in several surrounding cities. One of her favorite scriptures, Matthew 25:35, "For I was hungry, and you gave Me food; I was thirsty and you gave Me drink; I was a stranger and you took me in," embodies her heart for serving others.

Joyce and her husband have four wonderful children. Though she works full-time in the mental health industry, Joyce also balances her husband's full-time care after a sudden and catastrophic illness in June 2019. She is a relentless "God-chaser," walking with a joy that's everlasting.

KEILA VERA is one of the leaders that make up the Seeking God Club (SGC). After many trials and tribulations, she longed to discover who she was and what her purpose was. Keila enrolled in an online study called the Purpose Driven Life (PDL). It was then that she realized that without a relationship with God, she would not be able to live life with purpose. She repeated the study three times, then discovered her purpose. She turned her trials into testimonies and began to share in order to help others get through what seems impossible. Led to teach, Keila leads a small group bible study through her church as well as teaches the word of God through PDL online classes, living life on and with purpose.

Keila has a heart of giving and loves to help others. She has two young adult children, Zackery and Zoe, who have helped shape the life she is living today. She has an artistic gift and loves to craft, sing, and perform concerts when no one is watching. She loves to travel and explore different cultures. Keila believes that God's timing is perfect. One of her favorite scriptures is Jeremiah 29:11, New International Version, "'For I know the plans I have for you,' declares the Lord, 'plans to give you hope and a future.'"

MARIA RIVERA is a mother of two and grandmother of two boys. She is also a fulltime caregiver for her mother. In her role as a Seeking God Club leader, she is passionate about the Spanish ministry and desires to encourage others through the teachings of scripture, song, and lessons learned from personal life experiences. Saying "yes" to God during a difficult time in her life has produced unimaginable blessings and spiritual growth. A scripture that is close to her heart and has made a huge impact is Hebrews 13:5, "I will never leave you nor forsake you." Maria and her husband, Juan, have been married since 1986.

MIRIAN CUKOVIC became a born-again Christian in 2017 and her life changed. She decided to follow a call to get closer to Jesus, letting Him take control over her life. She walks in the great commission of Jesus's plan to bring the Word to others, specifically to her friends and especially her family. As a leader in the Seeking God Club and her involvement in a Spanish-speaking Bible study, she has been enriched with Bible knowledge and understanding, and for that, she is grateful.

Mirian proudly testifies, "One day, my sister Mayra decided to listen to a devotional I sent her while cleaning her house. Suddenly, her phone fell down and the recording stopped. She tried two times to continue listening without success, until she decided to sit down and listen to it from the beginning and the recording went all the way through. Mayra testified to me, 'Jesus showed me to stay still and listen to it from the beginning to the end,' and she was amazed. God is great and He will show you the way to get to the Father and rich salvation, not just for you but for your loved ones."

Mirian is married to Andre and has a son, Bekim, and a daughter, Nurija. Her family is a blessing in her life. Mirian's favorite scriptures are Psalm 31:3, "For you are my rock and my fortress; therefore, for your name's sake, lead me and guide me," and Psalm 32:8, "I will instruct you and teach you in the way you should go; I will guide you with My eye."

VENISS AGUILERRA is an Intercessor and as a leader with the Seeking God Club, she enjoys sharing the Word of God through teaching and praying. Veniss is also a Spiritual Leader with Spiritually Inspired Sisters (SIS). This ministry encourages women to pray more and develop a deeper and more intimate relationship with Christ. SIS also promotes and supports others to walk in their God-given purpose and develop the spiritual leader within.

Veniss is honored to be a part of this book because the Word of God and journaling her painful and tough experiences helped her to get through difficult times, which helped her to see what God is doing in her life. Reading and writing gives her strength and motivates her to keep growing closer to the Lord, and to take as many people with her as she can.

Veniss is a proud mother of four sons, Davion, Dylan, Damarion, and DaMontae. Veniss' go-to scriptures are James 1:2-4, "Consider it pure joy my brothers and sisters whenever you face trials of many kinds. Because you know that the testing of your faith produces perseverance. Let perseverance finish its work so that you may be mature and complete not lacking anything," and Deuteronomy 26:18, "And the Lord has declared today that you are a people for His treasured possession, as He has promised you, and that you are to keep His commandments."

VILMA TRICOCHE was baptized in 2002 and went to church every Sunday, but didn't have a relationship with God. In 2017, Vilma joined a virtual class called PDL that taught from the Purpose Driven Life book by Rick Warren. It was through this class that she became disciplined to get up early in the morning to pray and dedicate time with God. This led to her ability to confidently say that she has a close relationship with God. Vilma loves to read the Bible, daily devotionals, and praise God early each day.

Vilma gets much satisfaction as she operates through her gift of helping others. Volunteering at her church gives her joy. Additionally, she loves to help give the word of God to others in partnership with a wonderful group of prayer warriors in the Seeking God Club. She is one of the leaders that delivers the Word through the weekly SGC Spanish-speaking ministry.

Vilma has been married to her wonderful husband since 1992. Together, they have six grown adult children and presently a total of eleven grandchildren whom they adore. She loves spending time with them, as well as gardening in the summer. Her favorite Scripture is John 3:16, "For God so loved the world that He gave His one and only Son, that whoever believes in Him shall not perish but have eternal life."

Index

Made in the USA
Middletown, DE
14 April 2021

37644838R00129